Maximizing Your Money as an Uber® and Lyft® Driver

Make more money in less time!

© 2017, James Sutton Jr., Mount Holly, NC

ALL RIGHTS RESERVED. No part of this book may be reproduced or transmitted in any form or by any means without written permission from the author.

Disclaimer: Uber® and Lyft® are registered trademarks. The contents of this book are solely based on my experiences and research. Please verify all qualifications for your country, state, and county.

<u>**In Loving Memory**</u>

My Little Brother

Malik Sutton

My Cousin

Sean T. Nixon

My Uncle

Harvey Jarrett Sr.

It truly pains me to write any of these names but my baby brother Malik, three days before his 21st Birthday stings beyond belief – it hurts; a new father, about to graduate college… unexpected and untimely. My cousin Sean and Uncle Harvey both succumbed to the deadly disease of cancer. Family and friends, these past few weeks have been difficult… But

God! Let's remember the love, joy, and happiness each of these men brought into our lives... Gone but not Forgotten!

How do you break a stone, chisel away at it! The chips keep coming – let's hold each other up. Please don't bicker and fight – you can't measure the depth of someone else's love. You can't discount a caregiver, a mother, wife, significant other, a son, daughter, brother, sister or even a friend – I pray for your comfort, please pray for mine.

To God be the Glory

I give all honor to God who strengthens me and provides me with knowledge and direction. I thank you Lord for allowing me to reach others in a way that is unique and informative. Thank you for giving me the gifts, talents, and the ability to lead others and get results. All I do and all I will ever do is magnify You.

Jeannett

I thank my beautiful wife Jeannett; you are my rock; my rib! We have shared over 20 years together growing, learning, and loving. I thank you so much for being a praying woman of God. Your prayers have carried us and our children to unimaginable favor. Beyond your beauty and to your soul – I honor you. It is easy to imagine that God has only scratched the surface of the Blessings he has for us; ...because of you!

> He who finds a wife finds what is good
> and receives favor from the LORD.
> (NIV, Proverbs 18:22)

__Thanks Family__

I thank God for my children and grandchildren – doing better is the optimum word:

    Lemar, Janelle, Sasha, Malcolm, Jenae

Thank You God for our parents:

    James & Theresa
    John & Patricia

My brothers and sisters, you are all remarkable and you have all planted a seed in me to make me who I am today: Thank You!

    Kim, Sabrina, Louis, Todd, Malik
    Donna, Tondia, Precola, John Jr.

Forward

I told a close friend of mine from the block, I will call her "Flow" – "if we worked together, we would be millionaires because of my "Hustle"" -So I imagined what life would be like if "Hustle and Flow" were together. If you could go back to the block and do it all over again – What could your "Hustle & Flow" accomplish?

If you want to be successful in any business your hustle and flow must be in sync – The Hustle is the grind – the Flow is the plan. Hustle and Flow must be together – they are required to overcome adversity and leads to the formation of your "Grit" – Good Luck

Flow will always be the inspiration to my Hustle!

Table of Contents

Chapter 1:   Uber and Lyft Basics

Chapter 2:   Not just a J.O.B.

Chapter 3:   Servitude without the Attitude

Chapter 4:   James… Show Me the Money!

Chapter 5:   Get Referrals – Get Paid!

Chapter 5:   Safety

Chapter 6:   3 Step – 1 Page Recap

Chapter 7:   Rider Reviews

Chapter 1

Uber and Lyft Basics

"Treat it like a job until it pays like a business"

'Every job has a process but not everyone figures it out"
~ Jamesism

Drive!

If I were to begin and end this book with one word, for making money working with Uber and Lyft, I would begin and end the book with the word - "Drive"!

New Experience

When I started driving for Uber and Lyft, I found that most drivers that were not making the money they wanted, were not putting in the hours driving.

The ones putting in the excessive hours driving were not maximizing their time and effort.

Anyone 21 years and older with an authorized car & clean driving record, can become an Uber and/or Lyft driver. Anyone qualified can make money from being a ride-share driver with Uber and Lyft. Please make sure you check with your state and county for specific qualifications. The beautiful thing is it's not rocket science, but there is a science to maximizing the money you want to make. When I began this journey as a ride-share partner, I didn't know what to expect. I was introduced to Uber and Lyft about six-months before I started driving. My circumstance changed and I had to take the plunge. Quite honestly, I was lost when I began. If I had the benefit of a mentor/coach I would have started immediately. After speaking with various drivers,

I heard many horror stories about the company, their driving experiences, and their lack of making money. After conducting research and peeling back the onion, I saw an opportunity to capitalize on the experiences and mistakes made by other drivers. I decided to develop a plan so I didn't repeat the mistakes of those drivers that started before me. In this book, I share these experiences and best practices with you. I will be your driving mentor and share with you the best practices I learned to increase my earnings. I am partnering with you to "show you the money".

While conducting my research, I also heard some very positive stories from drivers; I picked their brains and I followed the guidance of the individuals making money in the business. There was a lot to learn about the different techniques and schedules drivers used to be successful. They shared how they picked their locations and when to turn on the applications; etc. It was a lot! I also noticed there was not a play book to help the new drivers. Yes, Uber and Lyft provide training videos and they both have great customer support - I needed something I could jump into at crunch-time without waiting. I needed a business plan for this business I was undertaking – this is how I birthed the book:

MAXIMIZING YOUR MONEY AS AN UBER/LYFT DRIVER

MAKE MORE MONEY IN LESS TIME!

As your partner, coach, and trainer. I show you how you can make more money driving with Uber and Lyft. One of the first people I helped was Mildred. She was a new acquaintance, working with me on another business venture. During our discussion, she told me she was a driver with Uber and Lyft. She shared with me that she worked with Uber and Lyft almost 3 years. I was surprised when she told me she only made about $300 dollars per week. When I shared with her my success, we stopped talking about our other venture and focused on how I made money driving for Uber and Lyft. She wanted to know my secrets – she wanted to know about the things I did to be successful. "Long story tolerable", after a week of her implementing the best practices I shared, she doubled her income. The best practices and techniques I will share with you work! They are Tried, Tested, and Proven!

I spoke with a bunch of experienced drivers, inexperienced drivers, and the riders to get information about the effectiveness of working with Uber and Lyft. The book is based on the driving and riding experiences shared from drivers and riders. I specifically spoke with the riders and drivers to discuss their riding and driving habits – many of the riders shared their ride stories and experiences to let me know this was in fact a great place to establish my business. In this book, I will show you how I established my successful business with Uber and Lyft; and how you can establish your business success with Uber and Lyft. It can work because it works.

Ride-Sharing

Uber and Lyft are host companies for ride-sharing platforms – unlike a traditional taxi, individuals use their personal or rented vehicle (in some states), to provide rides for their personal customers. Uber and Lyft are the most popular ride-sharing platforms for drivers with a host of new platforms on the horizon such as: Juno, Fasten, Fare, and Curb; there is no end in sight to the number of ride-share companies that will come on board. For the most part, the differences between Uber and Lyft and other ride-share companies is limited. All the ride-share company platforms routinely offer incentives for drivers to focus on their specific brand and platform. As a driver, you will need to stay abreast of individual opportunities and incentives presented by each platform; before being enticed to the promotion, "Do the Math"! The Uber and Lyft applications have similarities; however, it is important that you spend time with each application to learn the specific details associated with each platform. Each platform provides unique details to try to set themselves apart. I have included some screen shots from various pages from each app as I explain the details of maximizing your money. If you are wondering if you will make more money driving for either Uber and/or Lyft... it depends. How popular are Uber and Lyft in your community? When I show you the money, one aspect is to know your community and the territory you intend to cover.

My Story

As you read in my bio, I am a somewhat accomplished individual; both academically and in the professional world. I've held jobs from mailroom clerk to College President - I am here to tell you, if you love to drive and if you love to have great conversations this is the ultimate job. I have supervised hundreds of people while serving in the military and in corporate America - I've made hundreds of thousands a year in income; for me, this is by far one of the best jobs I've had in my career.

My Start-up Experience

My career as a driver partner with Uber and Lyft began by "happens chance." Unfortunately, I didn't begin this career on purpose, but I am truly happy it began. Consequently, I didn't have the benefit of this book or a platform to discuss how to be an effective driver. Prior to becoming a driver, I worked in the for-profit education industry; the industry is in the midst of change. I loved working with my students and staff; however, amid change, I was working with the worst manager of my career. I was putting in more than 70 hours per week (including my commute). With all that time vested, it still wasn't enough to get the job done; I was failing. On paper, I was making six figures but I was making much less with the number of hours I was working. I just said to myself – "Self" - Do the Math.

When I was let go from that position it was a blessing and a curse. The blessing was the immediate stress relief from working myself into the grave – being released gave me my life back. However, the curse was the loss of income. While my time was freed up, so were my pockets; it's not easy to replace 100k – or so I thought.

Own Your Time!

It's crazy to think about but giving myself back 30 hours per week has literally changed my life. When I say this is the best job I have had in 30 years, it is no exaggeration. The beautiful thing about working with Uber and Lyft is you are in control of your schedule. The best thing about making your own schedule is you own your time -

You can plan your schedule around the things you want to do. Whether you intend to work with Uber and Lyft full-time, part-time, or some-time, you own your time! I will show you how to maximize that time to make the maximum money!

Time Ownership

My dream has been to has been to spend more time giving back to the community - I now have the time and opportunity to reach out and empower young adults; and here I am reaching out to you. I've joined Toastmasters, I work with The Empowerment Duo and go to meetings at the Empowerment Center every Friday- I work with The Exchange Church - I own my time! Owning my time, allowed me to have more family time.

My daughter Jenae wanted to brush up on her driving skills before she took her driver's test – by being an Uber and Lyft Partner, I controlled my time. I could meet with her 2 hours every day for a month so she could get some driving in - she passed her test on the first try - there is no way I could have done that in any of my previous positions.

I've owned my home for the past 11 years - but for the first time ever, I could sit on my porch midweek and relax. I don't remember ever sitting on my porch sipping sweet tea midday - I own my time!

It's funny as I work to replenish my savings and pay back those that helped me in my time of need, with this business, I can literally ask my wife where she wants to "go out" to eat - and depending on the price point of the restaurant – Leave for a couple of hours, make money, to cover the dinner cost - Lol! Did I mention "I own my time!"

Personal Tour Guide

As an Uber and Lyft driver, I have become my own personal tour guide - after 11 years of living in my city, I thought I knew my city. Driving for Uber and Lyft have opened doors and windows to the unknown. I can literally say I visit new communities daily - when I drop riders off at restaurants, hotels, and events - I jot down the locations and events that interest me. I have a long list of restaurants to visit. I also learned about discount local vacation spots, community fairs, and events for my whole family. Did you know the best time to get to Crowders Mountain to avoid lines? I've picked up a 5 Star Chef that have given me invitations to his private table.

Amazing People

Speaking of people like that five-star chef - I have met some amazing people driving for Uber and Lyft - I've picked up a four-time Super Bowl champion - I picked up Raven Ferrell - she played Tupac's sister in "All Eyez on Me"; I helped Raven out during a layover and we are now friends on Instagram – She even spoke to my daughter on FaceTime'. I've met artist, singers, musicians, and my professional network has tripled.

Networking

Just to clarify a point I never discussed - I am an Uber and Lyft driver because I want to be an Uber and Lyft driver! When I was first let go from my job, I looked for jobs - what I found was Uber and Lyft are dynamic networking platforms.

When I started driving, I carried my resume with me. I drove near the airport and downtown areas so I could pick-up professionals… the movers and shakers. I picked up numerous hiring managers and executives. This gave me the opportunity to hand them my resume and I gave it to dozens of people. I was amazed at the number of call backs I received. I received more callbacks for interviews by driving Uber and Lyft then any job board I used during my job search including: Monster, Career Builder, ZIP Recruiter, and LinkedIn - I have met and continue to meet dozens of executives, hiring managers, and employees for many different companies - driving with Uber and Lyft gets you connected.

One of the most amazing offers I received by networking with Uber and Lyft was a position at Allstate; I was basically hired on the spot - unbeknownst to me, I was driving around a millionaire agency owner - he was looking, I was looking and after we talked, he gave me full access to his agency, an office, and leads!

I was offered a few other positions and two had six figure salaries! Because I wanted to own my time, I could pick and choose where I wanted to work. I recently partnered with a company that will pay me for my time and talents - I am a 5 Star Uber and Lyft driver with a few side-hustles. I got it all and I own my time! As you can see Uber and Lyft are more than the normal J.O.B. -it is truly a vehicle that can lead you to other opportunities.

Fear of Self-Employment

It's scary when you first venture out on your own to start a business. I was scared. Especially when your primary stream of income has stopped. Driving for Uber and Lyft is even more intimidating because of the personal nature of the business. You are picking up strangers, you are using your personal vehicle, and you are self-employed. This means if you don't work you don't eat. Back to the beginning... Drive. The beautiful thing about the Uber and Lyft systems, they are virtually a plug & play system.

No Upfront Cost

There are no upfront fees to start your business with Uber and Lyft. There is no direct marketing cost. There is no direct I.T. cost. There is very little overhead besides gas and time. In many cases, drivers already make car and insurance payments. Be mindful that your insurance company may increase your rates due to increased vehicle usage and you are responsible for paying your own self-employment taxes.

Uber and Lyft Percentage

Drivers make 80% on every fare. The money you receive as discussed in this book is based on your

80% share from Uber and Lyft - I already accounted for Uber and Lyft's 20% cost.

Uber and Lyft take out their share of about 20% per ride (in some markets the cost is higher); the 20% covers their operational cost such as: staffing, advertising, marketing, app development, legal representation, and other fees. This is a plug & play system so everything is taken care of for you. They are providing the platform and software. They must also keep the technology updated to be compatible with android and apple updates. We just need to focus on making money.

Sign-on Bonus

As a new driver, it is important for you to take advantage of the sign-on bonuses – I missed out on $350 dollars because it took me six months to jump in my car and drive. When you sign-up, use the below referral codes and I will assist you in maximizing your time and efforts to cash in on that bonus. Use these referral/bonus codes to sign-up:

Uber Referral/Bonus Code: CJTCWH78UE

Lyft Referral/Bonus Code: JAMES64330

The beautiful thing about using my code is I will support you and Uber and Lyft will pay me a referral fee for introducing you to the business. – It's a win-win!

Signing Up

Signing up to drive for Uber and Lyft is as simple as signing up for a Facebook account. If you have a car that meets the qualifications (check each company to verify the current qualifications). You enter your driver's license and insurance information; they do the background checks and you are in. When I signed up for the Lyft Driver Partner, I met with an Lyft associate whom inspected my vehicle and took me on a test drive. Uber just verified my information. Take a moment to sign-up – If you are on one platform, sign-up for the other to take advantage of the current bonus. Don't forget to use my referral/bonus code:

Uber Referral/Bonus Code: CJTCWH78UE

Lyft Referral/Bonus Code: JAMES64330

Elite Driver Program

Both Uber and Lyft have elite driver platforms such as: Uber Black and Lyft Lux & SUV. I can assist drivers on all levels, but this book is geared toward Uber XL and Lyft drivers. However, the best-practices can be applied to every level. The basic difference between the elite driver platforms are the clientele and the luxury car requirements.

Your Personal Operating Cost

You need to figure out your operating cost - know the wear and tear on your car, how much it will cost for you to own and operate your car. You must account for your IRS deductions – If you get a basis understanding of the IRS mileage rate and expenses, you can save a lot of money.

Retired Military

This is the perfect job for military retirees or retirees in general - As retirees you already have medical benefits - a pension and time. I found that some of the older drivers enjoy working because they enjoy driving and talking. I had a passenger comment about her enjoyable ride with an elderly woman – The rider stated, "she was comforting and energetic."

I recently met with a retiree driver and he wanted to increase his earnings. We discussed some of the things he was doing in his business. After a brief discussion and a few tweaks, he increased his income by 25% - in dollars that's about 200 dollars per week. It met his personal goal.

Walkthrough

The Lyft app provides potential driver with a simulated walkthrough. This allows drivers to get a mock ride and go through the motions of accepting and dropping off a rider. I highly encourage you to work with the application from both Uber and Lyft – become a passenger and experience it from both sides. The operation for both Uber and Lyft are the same so if you walk through the Lyft App you will find them both simulator. Uber has a great training video on YouTube at https://youtu.be/JvEFw2AGLOw

Chapter 2

It's Not just a J.O.B.

"When you use my system, you will not be Just Over Broke" ~ Jamesism

> For the life of me, I will never understand how I was able to put in 70 hours a week (including commute) for my job but I can't muster up 20 hours a week for myself ~ Jamesism

It's more than a J.O.B.

Welcome to the world of 1099's – with independence comes great responsibility. It's more than a job, it's your business. The bottom-line... if you don't work, you don't eat.

I told you my why in the first chapter of this book - now you should define your why. The biggest misconception I hear from other Uber and Lyft drivers are they don't need a business plan; or in simpler terms they don't need a plan of action. I have always lived by the mantra "plan your work and work your plan" - I have run into countless professionals that had great plans but lacked execution and follow-through. My first week as a driver, I realized without a concrete plan I would not make the money I desired. My first week I chased rides, by week two rides chased me. Following the tips and best-practices I outline throughout this book – you won't have to be a ride chaser. As you begin this venture you need to define your expectations and know your goal; both monetarily and time. Is this a part-time business, full-time business, or a means to an end? Most importantly, you need to plan how you intend to achieve your goal.

Understanding Your Why

Everyone's why is different, but their objective is the same; to make money. My take-home pay in my previous position was $2600 every two weeks - my goal was income replacement- I had to take home $1300 per week and factor in taxes to be paid at the end of the quarter. To increase my income, I had to think about ways to maximize my time and effort. If I could put 70 hours in for someone else, surely, I could do just as much for myself.

Why Drive?

If you are using Uber and Lyft while you find a job, to get some part-time cash, or if you are thinking about driving full-time. Take some time to define your "why" and work to develop the perfect program for you to make the maximum money.

Getting Paid

The first thing you must know out the gate is how you are paid - how do you make money driving for Uber and/or Lyft - the beautiful thing is you don't have to run a magic formula to do the math; 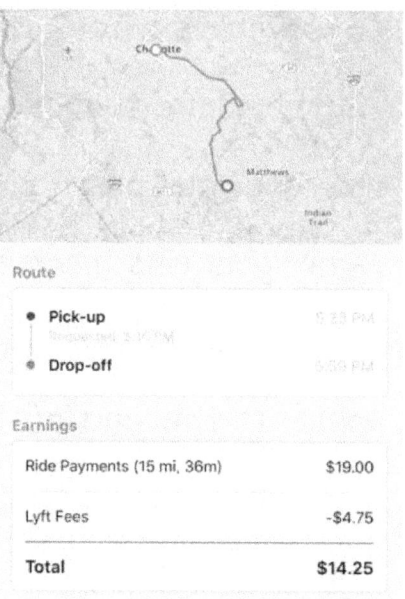 it's done for you. However, it's important for you to know what factors into your payment and how payments are calculated for your payout. Both Uber and Lyft provide a detailed breakdown of earnings for every ride. Your payout is based on your 80% split 😊.

The lowdown is simple... it is basically 12 cents per minute wait time and about 67 cents per mile – the simple math is you want miles! Look at your statement to see and calculate the actual per ride amounts and to see the breakdown of all payout details.

I highly encourage you to spend some time looking at the numbers - that basic knowledge is enough to give you confidence that you can make money driving - at the end of the day, the focus will be location, location, timing, planning, and location. Where are the rides and how do you position yourself to get them?

Once you understand the basics of earnings, the process turns into meeting your daily income expectations. Remember, if you don't work, you don't eat!

Work Schedule

I strongly suggest you create a work schedule. Being self-employed does not mean you don't put in a minimum of 40 hours - the beauty of being independent is you decide when the 40 hours are worked to get the maximum return for your business. You choose the number of hours you work, the time you work, and the best location to work to maximize your earnings. You set your income expectations and then put in the work to meet that goal. Being independent simply means you are your own boss – it doesn't mean you do not work. You must "treat it like a job, until it pays like a business." You need to continuously remind yourself "if you don't work, you don't eat". You must know how many hours it will take for you to get to your bottom line.

My schedule is as follows (some flexibility):

Monday – Wednesday 0800 am – 6 p.m.

Thursday & Friday 6 p.m. – Midnight

Saturday, I work as needed to achieve my goal, to cover special events, or to make extra money. Yes, sometimes I work some long days; there is no limit to the number of hours you can work outside of driver safety,

The best time to drive is when riders need rides such as: morning commutes, afternoon and evening rush hour, after work drinks, and early morning bar closings. The is a mantra in this business to "follow the alcohol" - if they are serving drinks, riders need rides!

You Serve!

You are in the service industry and you must work service industry schedules. You must drive when people need rides.

Income Goals

I always have income goals associated with my schedule. For example, Monday - Wednesday my income goals are $150 per day - by Wednesday, I needs to be at $450 dollars - If I am not at my production goals, I schedule myself for overtime – Also, if I fall short on the number of hours I work per week, for whatever reason, I readjust my schedule. On Thursday – Saturday, my goal is $200 per night- When I work a full work week with no distractions – I typically make between $1000 – 1500 dollars. To increase my income, I do in fact increase my hours.

I have met drivers that work a variety of shifts – the only advice I would provide is be consistent. If you have a set schedule it makes it easier to track your progress.

We will discuss peak times and performance in a later chapter. We will also dig into the details of maximizing your income - but first you have to have an understanding of being in business - right now the focus will be on when you are paid, tracking your rides, and understanding all aspects of payments. These things combined will affect your bottom line.

Payday

The beautiful thing about being a rideshare partner with Uber and Lyft, you get paid every day. At the end of every shift you have the option of having funds deposited directly into your bank account. This means you can wake up broke, with a quarter of gas in your tank, and end the day cash out $200 dollars. Just cash-out and refill your tank with your first few rides of the day.

Here are a few examples of pay-out potential:
If you work 40 hours per week and take in a minimum of $15 dollars per hour – You take home $600 dollars. You make approximately $1 dollar per mile so that is approximately 600 miles; at 53 cents per mile that is $318 dollars as a tax

deduction – so of the $600 – approximately $282 is taxable income.

If you make $1000 per week, approximately $500 is tax deductible with your mileage tracking. Please note these are estimates and your true income will be determined by how much you drive, how many miles you drive, and how much time you drive, and if you use a great system.

Caution:

As a business owner don't make a habit of spending every dime you earn. As an independent contractor, you are responsible for paying your own taxes so plan accordingly. Please go to irs.gov and look up self-employment taxes.

Mileage Tracker

I find it important to track my miles. The better record keeping you do, the easier it will be for you to complete your quarterly and yearly taxes. There are several apps available to track your mileage, income, and expenses. I use QuickBooks Self-Employed. https://selfemployed.intuit.com

There are quite a few apps available that can track your mileage and expenses but self-employed is my preference. This app also serves as a daily reminder that I am indeed self-employed. As you begin setting goals for your business remember, if you don't work, you don't

eat. Having your personal mileage tracker will help give you a clear indication of your yearly and quarterly tax-deduction. Uber and Lyft will provide you with an end of year statement 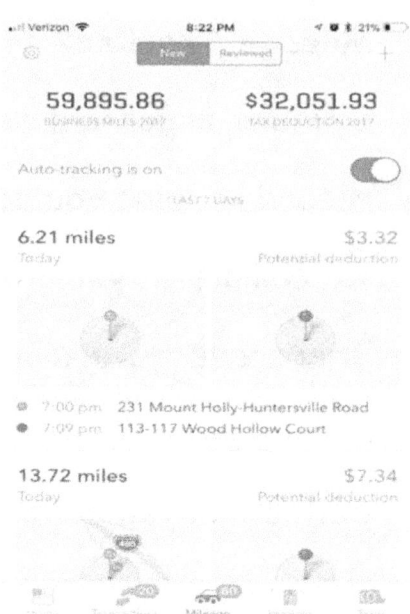 showing your earnings and mileage. You should also track your own daily, weekly, monthly, quarterly, and yearly mileage. Uber and Lyft does not account for all your miles driven. Their mileage doesn't account for the time you drive to an area to start accepting rides. I've met several drivers that have left thousands of dollars on the table because they did not claim all their mileage; 53 cents per mile adds up. By using a mileage tracker, you will be able to see your mileage, expenses, and deposits from both ride-share platforms in one location.

Time Off

Don't forget to plan for and consider time-off due to vacation and illness. You may also want to consider vehicle down time and personal rest periods. You can also have multiple cars registered to your account for Uber and Lyft; this is great to cover you in emergencies so you can keep earning. This is your business so you must account for unforeseen circumstances. If I schedule planned time-off, I extend my work hours the previous two-weeks to offset earnings for the time missed. Additionally, I plan my schedule and income based on 50 weeks per year vs. 52 weeks per year; this allows for a two-week planned vacation and/or sick days. I still use the Five-P's; Proper, Planning, Prevents, Poor, Performance.

Tracking Expenses

The beautiful thing about driving with Uber and Lyft is your everyday overhead expenses are limited to gas and time. In many cases, the car payment and insurance were already a part of your monthly bills. There may be an increase in gas usage and vehicle preventive maintenance will be performed more frequently; be mindful to track these costs. Do the math!

Understanding Vehicle Usage

One area of concern I hear from drivers or potential drivers is the increased mileage they will put on their car. You are a business owner working on a 1099 – your mileage is tax deductible. You can make 4 times the car payment every month, with the mileage deduction, your vehicle practically pays for itself. To date, my tax deduction will be more than the total cost of my car. Do the math!

If you downloaded your mileage tracker you are ready to move on to the next step.

Chapter 3

Servitude w/o the Attitude

"The customer is always right but do not have all the answers"" ~ Jamesism

Welcome to the Service Industry

This is your business – take time to prepare.

Driver Daily Preparation

1. Driver appearance and hygiene

2. Clean your vehicle - Febreze after every ride.

3. Prepare your snacks and drink

4. Turn on your driver partner app

5. Do a checkup from the neck up! Your attitude matters 99% of the time. The 1% is during your restroom break.

6. Ask for the Referral

Customer Service

Welcome to the wonderful world of customer service. You work in the service industry, so your hours should reflect service industry hours. The peak time for the service industry venues such as: Hotels, Bars, Restaurants, and Airports are during the arrival and departure times of guest. Additionally, consider local events going on in your community such as street fairs and services. Uber does a great job of letting drivers know about major events in the community. However, it is not an all-inclusive list. Spend some time planning your drives as you would any other business.

Surrounding Area

Riders must get to their scheduled events on time. Having a general idea of the background and demographics of your community will position you to bring people to the event as well as bring them home.

Servitude without the Attitude

If you never worked in the service industry the process is simple "The customer is always right but do not have all the answers" - no they don't - as a server, it is your job to insure your customer's experience is 5 stars! When I drive, I represent myself, Uber and Lyft, and all the other drivers providing this service. My actions impact the desire for riders to continue to use this service.

As a server, you must gage your customer. When you arrive for a pickup, verify upon arrival if the rider needs assistance; if they need help, help!

Surprising Revelation

I've spoken to many drivers that don't believe in going the extra mile - outside of tips and driver ratings - in the service industry going the extra mile is the standard. Personally, I enjoy reading my customer reviews. It confirms I am doing a great job and most importantly, I am doing it right! Your attitude and positive energy is contagious - I know some drivers have snacks and drinks – others have phone chargers or access to music - at the end of the day nothing beats your positive energy and personality. I get quite a bit of customer feedbacks; 90% are about the conversation and my positive personality.

Driver Profile

Uber and Lyft allow you to post a personal profile! I have found many riders view the profile prior to getting picked up by their driver. You only get one chance to make a first impression – your profile is your blind date. I look at the riders' profile to get a general idea of who they are; most riders profiles are just generic, but I want mine to set the tone. It starts with the first impression - your profile picture and driver profile. Take a few minutes to make sure you are starting this relationship on the right foot. Many riders review drivers' profiles to determine whether to accept or decline a driver.

Five Star Rating

Your driver rating is critical to maintaining a great relationship with Uber & Lyft. It can also impact your rider acceptance. There is a lot riding on whether you provide a 5 Star experience. We want all riders to continue to use the service. We need all riders

Rider thank you notes

❝ James is a very intelligent man and holds great conversation. He seems to really care about his customers and is a driver that gives Uber a good name! Thanks again James!

❝ Great driver. Loved the IPad with my name on it...in the dash when he pulled up...so I could see this was my ride. Brilliant

❝ There are many great Uber drivers. Nearly everyone I ride with is good, but James is the best of the best.

❝ I really enjoyed my ride, great enlighten conversation. I'm very thankful that I met such a great person.

❝ Thank you for the great conversation and ride. Very well prepared for anything; Even the Solar Eclipse.

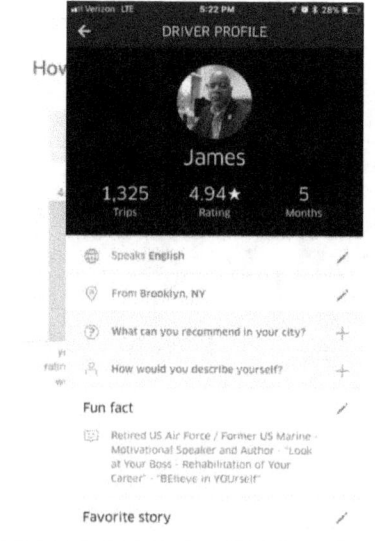
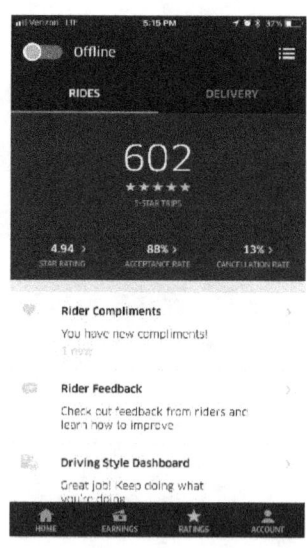

referring other riders to use the platforms. Our job security relies on the experience you provide for every rider. Additionally, getting tips and 5 stars ratings go hand and hand. I found riders that like you and rate you well, tip you well. Poor customer service will guarantee a poor rating and no tip!

Note: To remain active with Uber and Lyft you must maintain the appropriate 4.6 or above Star Rating.

Compliments Matter

I love the comments section for both Uber and Lyft. Uber keeps them on their platform and Lyft emails them out to you daily. I know when I read my comments its validation that I am providing great customer service. I thrive to maintain my perfect rating and I know it reflects the effort I put in for all rides.

Tipping

At the end of ride, happy customers tip! If you're looking for a way to increase your income without adding additional hours, then provide great service and capitalize on tips.

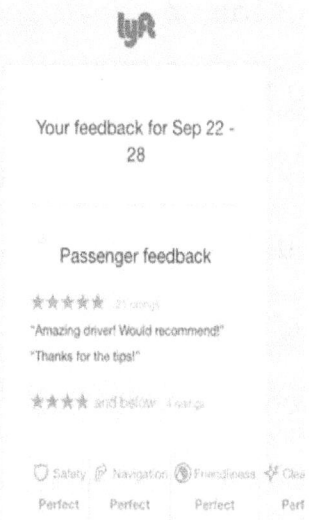

Clean Cars

The next thing is your vehicle - regardless of the year, make, and model of your car - it should be clean and serviceable. Wash and/or wipe down your vehicle daily and throughout the day. This will also cut down on germs as you encounter dozens of people daily in a closed environment. I've picked up countless customers that have complimented me on the cleanliness of my vehicle as they recapped the negative experiences they had with other drivers. I keep Febreze in my car and spray after almost every ride - especially if I have a customer with a B/O or carrying food. I don't allow eating or drinking in my car but sometimes people get in with lunch to go. If you take pride in your presentation it will reflect in your tips and driver ratings.

AC and Heat

I have had riders share their drivers did not use AC and/or Heat during their ride. Drivers, your rider's comfort is paramount. Without the basic amenity of AC and Heat you are guaranteeing yourself a low rating. Based on the rider responses, each driver that failed to provide basic comforts received negative ratings. If you are not sure ask. Even if you have a malfunction – talking to your client may prevent the negative rating.

Personal Hygiene

When you work in a close-proximity of people you must be aware of your personal hygiene – Go the extra mile – freshen up from time to time throughout the day. Keep deodorant and a cool rag nearby; from time to time, get out the car and air out. If you have not heard of the term "Monkey Butt" look it up. It doesn't sound pleasant because it's not pleasant; especially for your rider.

The Greeting

When I pull up to greet my customers, their name is displayed on my dashboard. I use an app called "hail me" for my iPad – and "signboard" for android tablets. I put my iPad on my dashboard and display my rider's name. This action has increased my ratings and tips tenfold. It also puts riders at ease because they know you are there to pick them up. It is especially useful at the airport and large events.

Initial Interaction

Once the customer is in your car, ask if the temperature and music are OK. Some drivers prefer to not allow riders music access; I don't mind. It's ok to allow the customer to set the mood. If you are out on a Friday night –playing your favorite slow jam CD, it might not be the right music to set the tone – Personally, I listen to whatever music the customer wants to listen to during the ride. I go the extra mile! When I pick up someone going to a concert or event, I'll play the music of the artist performing. Wherever we are heading, I will make sure that I have that music on tap to get the customer in an enjoyable mood. I recently dropped two young ladies off at a J. Cole concert and they were ecstatic I had J. Cole playing on the way to the concert. Listening to my customer's tunes for 5 or 10 minutes during a ride, will not make or break my day but it can enhance the customer experience and my tip.

Conversation Exchange

You may not be the ultimate conversationalist... So, it may be difficult for you to engage and interact with your customers. However, that is an important part of your job. Just like a bartender or anyone that works in the customer service field, engaging with customers is critical. Some basic questions like:

How was your day?

What type of work do you do?

Are you visiting? From Where – basically let the conversation will flow.

If your riders ask you questions – try to answer – start the conversation with the basic questions – have fun - know your why –why do you drive. Most importantly show your enthusiasm about what you do – Happy Drivers get good ratings, tips… and referrals. You must know when to turn it on and off, but the more you drive the more you will know about your customer needs. However, don't make assumptions, let the conversation flow naturally.

To Speak or Not Speak

If a customer does not want to talk – don't talk. Sometimes you may encounter a customer that doesn't want to talk; that's ok; shut-up and drive. There will always be indicators that a customer doesn't want to talk, a clear indicator is when they put their headphones on. Sometimes you may get a passenger that just sits and gives you a blank stare; that's ok. More times than not, you will get customers that want to engage and converse – they want to talk about their day and they want to hear about your day. Be mindful if your customer is on the phone or just not in the mood to hear any music at all. That is why it is a good practice to ask at the beginning of the ride. Your preparation is one key to making money and staying in good standing with the Uber and Lyft platforms.

Chapter 4

James... Show Me the Money!

"If there is liquor being served... your presence is needed!" ~ Jamesism

Making Money Today

Drive! Get in your car, turn on the application, and drive. If you turn on either app or both apps today you will make money. Uber and Lyft took care of all the marketing and IT cost. You just have to turn on the applications and drive.

Get Your Bonus

You must take advantage of the sign-on bonus! The Lyft bonus is up to $500 dollars – that number will vary - however, no matter what it is, that is your first option to making money. I repeat... As a new driver, it is important for you to take advantage of the sign-on bonus – I missed out on $350 dollars because it took me six months to jump in my car and drive. Don't miss out on your bonus! Go ahead and sign-up using the below referral/bonus codes. I will assist you in maximizing your time and efforts to cash in on that bonus. Use these referral codes to sign-up:

Uber Referral Code: CJTCWH78UE

Lyft Referral Code: JAMES64330

Yes, Uber and Lyft will pay me a referral fee for introducing you to the business. – the beautiful thing is I will show you how to benefit from referrals payments too. It's a win-win!

The World of 1099

The beautiful thing about being a 1099 in a noncompete arena you can work for multiple sources to include: Uber, Lyft, Postnotes, Uber Eats, Juno, etc. Managing multiple platforms can be tricky and overwhelming. It can be done but it takes practice and patience. Most importantly it requires you put the customer first. A rider on the other end of the request needs to get to a specific location; at a specific time.

Dual Application Process

When you are using both the Uber and Lyft applications to get rides, it increases your chances to get riders. I use both Uber and Lyft at the same time. I must admit it was a little tricky at first but I have come up with a simple routine to limit dual request:

1. Accept the first request immediately.
2. Switch over to the other app and turn it off.

3. Switch back to accepted app and navigate to pick-up location.
4. If you happen to get two request within seconds of each other, accept the first and cancel ths second.
5. It's important to stay true to the customer. Don't keep two acceptances because the rider is trying to get somewhere, give another driver the opportunity to fill the ride; this keeps the customer experience positive.
6. Be mindful of your acceptance rate – if you are cancelling rides make sure you are staying over 90% acceptance on both platforms.
7. Turn the other application back on when you are a minute out from your drop-off.

Developing a Schedule

The beautiful thing about being an Uber and Lyft driver is your control of your work schedule. You pick your work location and you decide whether or not to give someone a ride. But the true key to making money is putting together a strategic plan to maximize your time and effort. It requires research and it requires you to know your community. I know drivers that travel a hour away to maximize their income. Tracking surges and activity is the best way to determine the optimum time to drive.

You are in the service industry and the best time to find riders are when services are being rendered:

Rush Hour

Dinner Time

After Work

After Hours

Bar Closings

Before Concerts

After Concerts

Community Events

Typically, Uber provides a list of upcoming events on it's app; but you should check the local papers to see if a specific club or bar is having a special event. The more you know about your community the better. The simple rule of thumb is "If there are adult beverages being served… your presence is needed!"

Airport Rides:

I've met many riders that like to work the airport. I recommend the airport to individuals that are nervous about beginning a career as a driver. The airport is the safest drives because almost everyone has to go through security. Airport drivers are required to get additional training and in some cases purchase a permit. I typically don't work the airport because of the number of drivers working. When I decide to work the airport, I look at the arrival schedule and number of drivers in the "que" to decide if it will be profitable for me. The "airport driver que" is a system that both Uber and Lyft use to assign the next driver for a rider terminal pick-up – in my city, we have a designated parking lot – as drivers pull into the lot, they are automaticaaly assigned a place in line to be the next driver. The Uber and Lyft ques are separate so your number may be different for each platforms. I also use my surge tracker to pinpoint the best times to work my airport schedule. Planning airport time is critical to avoid excessive wait-times for the next ride.

Airport Goldmine:

I have been very efficient with tracking my rides "to" the airport. My philosophy was for every rider coming in to the airport, one was going out. I found that Thursday afternoons, Friday mornings and afternoons are primetimes for rides to the airport. I also track the location I drop riders off from the airport – it's a means they will eventually need a ride back to the airport. It's ok to ask your riders when they plan to go back to the airport, when does the conference or event they are attending ends, this helps you position yourself for return rides to the airport. I plan my day – it doesn't just happen.

Monitor Arrivals

One final tip, when working at the airport, you must monitor the arrival schedule. I use the arrival schedule on a slow day in the commmunity,

I check the number of arriving flights for each hour. I then look at the number of drivers in the "airport driver que" waiting on rides. I have found if there are twenty or more aircraft landing within the hour, the "airport driver que" moves quickly. This is a trial and error process and you have to figure out the best use of your time at the airport. The airport is also a good location to take your lunch – it keeps you primed for business and provides a 30 – 45 minute break.

Surge Pricing

During periods of high demand, all ride-share platforms including Uber and Lyft increase a drivers earning potential. I have seen surges as high as 400 percent. This means a $4 dollar ride pays out at $20 dollars. Do the Math!

The Surge Temptation

When you first start driving it is tempting to "chase the surges" but you will find the surge light dimming the closer you get to the location. On my second day out, I started journaling the surges to see if there was a hidden rhythm that would put me in the midst of the surge before it was activated.

Good Surge

There are some good surges such as special events and when the nightlife is in full effect. If there is alcohol being served, there is a need for our services.

Bad Surge

I only say "bad surge" because rookies have a tentancy to "chase surges" – All surges are good because there is more money available for rides. When I began driving for Uber and Lyft, I had no plan. I didn't know where the money was or how to get to it. When I looked at the map I saw red blotches for 50% up to 300% surges - I didn't know how to get to it – and when I arrived on scene the surges disappeared.

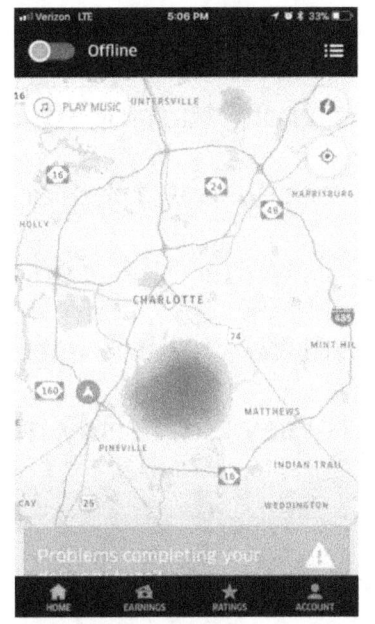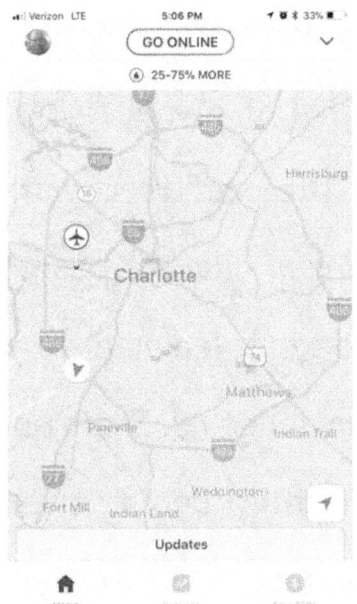

Journaling Surges

That's when I decided to start tracking my business and journaling my surges. I found that surges typically happen the same time every day at the same location. For instance, during rush hour surges happen at the same time and the same place every day. So, for about two weeks I tracked every time I saw a surge and I would put it on my calendar. I used a simple process to track my surges. When I saw a surge I created a calendar event with the location and time. I took control of my business and from that point on I saw the profits I wanted; because I treated my business like a business I made the funds I needed. I learned to capitalize on my time and financial gains. I can honestly say I am truly happy with this decision and I have no doubt in my mind that you can be just as happy and accomplished.

2 PM Surge Huntersville
3 PM University Uber
4 PM
5 PM Airport Rush
6 PM 150% Sharon Road
7 PM

Let me repeat – "Tipping"

At the end of ride, happy customers tip! If you're looking for a way to increase your income without adding additional hours, then provide great service and capitalize on tips.

There's More!

It's important that you revisit your journaling if the flow of rides or surges don't stay true to the documented times and dates. Data does not lie, follow the data. The surges are simply a way for Uber and Lyft to ensure there are enough drivers around to pick up the customers. They have their strategy so it is important that you have yours.

Like any business, you become aware of the areas that work for you – I have a set routine and after every drop-off I head back to my money maker location. I stay true to my work schedule because if I don't work, I don't eat.

Sneak Peek at Competition

You can use the Uber and Lyft Rider app to see where other drivers are located. On rare occassions, I take a sneak peek at my driver competition by logging in as a rider. This allows me to see if the location I am in is satuarated with other drivers. It typically doesn't matter in high traffic areas or at special events. I track my progress and the lack of progress by being familiar with the times and places of my successes and failures. Knowing when the other drivers are positioned assist me with my daily planning.

Guaranteed Rates

Lyft offers guaranteed rates to entice drivers to use their app over the competition's - if you're in the area that has higher usage, you don't lose anything or gain anything by not having both apps on.

Ride to Destination

Both platforms offer a ride to destination so drivers can control where they choose to pick up rides. I typically use the ride to destination feature when I am heading home or if I had a trip out of my normal zone to get me back on track. I've also talked to drivers that use this application to enhance their income and keep them in designated areas.

Lyft Streaks

This pays drivers premium bonuses for staying logged in to catch a series of rides.

Lyft seems to focus more on getting the drivers attention by offering huge bonuses and innovative ways to earn – look for more new updates.

Chapter 5

Get Referrals – Get Paid!

"another source of income"

Referrals

Referrals equate to free money! As a driver, you will meet hundreds of people a week. Many of the riders, their friends and/or family members may be looking for part-time or full-time employment. They heard your story, they have seen the commercials, and you have provided a positive insight. Now they are thinking about becoming a ride-share partner with Uber and/or Lyft Driver. If you let them exit the car without your referral code - you have done a great service for Uber and Lyft but you did not get compensated. In every sales position I held in my career, referrals were always the key to making more with less effort.

You Must Ask for the Referral

It is imperative that you give them your referral codes – which is why I give each rider my business card. Not only do I ask for the referral - I ask for the five-star rating and tip indirectly; directly!

Introduce people to the business. If you have ten referrals working a week, you increase your earnings by about a hundred dollars per week. The beautiful thing about referrals is they can come from anywhere and everywhere. Just give out your code so when they sign up, you get the credit. The person that introduced me to Uber and Lyft didn't get the referral bonus because she didn't leave me with her code. I wasn't thinking about her when I signed up. But when you give out your information – they have it and they are thinking about you and your experience – you want potential drivers thinking about you! Here is my code again for your benefit – sign-up and get in line for your bonus:

Uber Referral Code: CJTCWH78UE
Lyft Referral Code: JAMES64330

This is a sample of how Lyft will show you how your referrals pay out:

Sample Referral Payout from Lyft

887-69

Lyft earnings update: Yesterday you got $14.00 because your referral, Matt, gave 4 rides. Refer new drivers: http://lft.to/refer

Wednesday 1:04 PM

Lyft earnings update: Yesterday you got $7.00 because your referral, Matt, gave 2 rides. Refer new drivers: http://lft.to/refer

Friday 1:02 PM

Lyft earnings update: Yesterday you got $7.00 because your referral, Matt, gave 2 rides. Refer new

Chapter 6

Safety

"Get home to your family"

Once your customers are comfortable, the only thing you should do now is "drive safe and be safe".

Driver Safety

Think safe, be safe is something we use to say when I was in the Air Force. Both Uber and Lyft have things in place to help drivers be safe. All riders register with the user application and input credit card information etc. Some riders have pictures on their profiles but not all riders have their picture - Occasionally, you will get riders that use someone else's profile; validate the name. For your safety, validate each rider.

Identity Verification

Verify the identity of each rider prior to them getting in your car. The riders are told to verify your license plate number but typically they just hope in the car. As I stated earlier, I use my tablet to display the name of my rider when I arrive for pick-up. If you work the bar scene you may get an ambitious rider that just jumps in your car - politely let them know their vehicle is on the way.

Stay-Fit and Stretch

Get out of your car every hour or so and stretch. Walk around and keep your muscles relaxed. Drink water – and carry snacks. Keep the food choices healthy and odorless. I also keep light weight to keep my arms in motion.

Stranger Danger - On some occasions, you may pick up a minor - if I pick up someone under 16, I call at pick up and prior to signing out at drop-off.

Car Cam

I know numerous drivers that have installed car cameras - check your state laws and contracts to verify the legal ramifications.

Uber Identity Verification

Uber does random identity checks via facial recognition checks - and they recently installed a Peace of Mind action that allows your loved ones to track your rides and locations. Stay in touch!

Vehicle Safety

We talked about the need for a clean vehicle - cleanliness "as a whole" is important. It is just as important for you to operate a safe vehicle. You must inspect your vehicle daily - tire pressure -

turn signals - headlights - brakes lights - and windshield wipers.

Increased routine maintenance is important due to the increased vehicle usage.

Uber - Peace of Mind

This allows drivers to share their location with loved ones with a simple text message. Additionally, some drivers may want to take other precautions so someone knows where they are located at all times.

Uber Trip Sharing

Uber also allows drivers to share their trips with anyone they designate. Your love ones can follow you on every trip.

Life360

One app that I use track to my location is called Life360 - this app comes with an emergency alert to reach all contacts associated with the account. With Life360 you can add as many people as you want to notify in case of emergency.

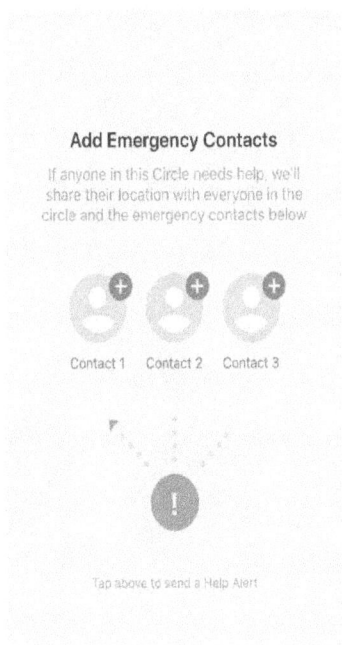

Chapter 6

3 Step 1-page Driver - Re-cap

"5 P's - Proper Planning Prevents Poor Performance"

Plan - Prepare - Drive!

Plan!
Set a work schedule
Track Surges
Know your territory and community

Prepare!
Personal Hygiene
Clean Car
Customer Interaction

Drive!
Think Safe, Be Safe
Verify Rider Identify
Inspect your vehicle

Chapter 7

Rider Reviews

"feel good moments – feel good"

"James was amazing! I love the name on the dashboard."
★ ★ ★ ★ ★
September 2017

"Thank u for getting my daughter to school safely!"
★ ★ ★ ★ ★
September 2017

"Best drive of my life!"
★ ★ ★ ★ ★
September 2017

"James thanks for the information on how to double my profits."
★ ★ ★ ★ ★

"Awesome driver!!!"
★ ★ ★ ★ ★
August 2017

"Thanks very much James!!"
★ ★ ★ ★ ★
August 2017

"Excellent person!"
★ ★ ★ ★ ★
August 2017

"Thank you for the great conversation and ride. Very well prepared for anything; Even the Solar Eclipse."
★ ★ ★ ★ ★
August 2017

Passenger feedback

★ ★ ★ ★ ★
"Thank you."
"Great person!Had fun with the conversation."
"All the above"

Safety – Perfect | Navigation – Perfect | Friendliness – Perfect | Cleanliness – Perfect

Passenger feedback

★ ★ ★ ★ ★
"Awesome ride!"
"Very polite & accommodating. Pleasantly surprised to see that he set up cartoons on his tablet for my kids to watch."

Safety – Perfect | Navigation – Perfect | Friendliness – Perfect | Cleanliness – Perfect

"Nice gentleman"

★★★★★
August 2017

"Thank you for such a professional and relaxed ride!"

★★★★★
August 2017

"Great driver. Loved the IPad with my name on it...in the dash when he pulled up...so I could see this was my ride. Brilliant"

★★★★★
August 2017

"Best uber ride ever. So much attention to detail and an amazing

"Best uber ride ever. So much attention to detail and an amazing conversationalist"

★★★★★
August 2017

"best uber ride ever. he's a really awesome person and it's probably the most fun car ride i've had"

★★★★★
July 2017

"Thank u so much !"

★★★★★
July 2017

"Great conversation!! Wonderful person."

Passenger feedback

★★★★★ 21 ratings
"He was genuinely ind"
"We thoroughly enjoyed our ride and conversation with James. He was so interesting!"
"Very professional. Nice conversation! James is the best!"

Safety | Navigation | Friendliness | Cleanliness
Perfect | Perfect | Perfect | Perfect

Passenger feedback

★★★★★ 28 ratings
"Thank you for getting him back safely!"
"Really fun conversationalist. Helped with my 'bags.' Would most definitely ride again. Thank You!"

★★★★ and below 3 ratings

Safety | Navigation | Friendliness | Cleanliness
Perfect | Perfect | Perfect | Perfect

Make Money, Own your Time!

About the Author

James Sutton Jr. is an author and impactful speaker. He conducts workshops in resume writing, effective communication, interviewing skills, and 21st Century job search. He has a passion to assist people in achieving their goal – thus his speeches are impactful as opposed to just motivational – he knows how to boost the morale of any organization.

James is a 23 year Retired United States Air Force and Marine Corps Veteran. He is the recipient of 'The Airman's Medal' for Heroism. He served as a College President & Director for two colleges, as well as, Director of Admissions for both campuses as well. James has over 30 years' experience in recruitment and personal development.

Purchase your book at my website:
www.jamessuttonjr.com
These titles are available as well:
"Look at Your Boss; Rehabilitation for Your Career"
"Effective Leaders: Mentor People & Manage Processes"
"BElieve in YOUrself"
"Preparing Teens & Young Adults for the Professional World"

Special Acknowledgement
Brian K. & Lisa Santiago McNeill
The Empowerment Duo

After one consultation, I felt truly empowered! You saw my vision and by the end of the day you sent me a cover that put my efforts on overdrive. Then within 2 days we launched our plan. Thank you both for the support and allowing me to bring this idea to fruition.

If you are an aspiring author, salesperson, or just someone with a dream, I would highly recommend *The Empowerment Duo* to help jumpstart your idea!

I want to add a special thank you to Lisa for the magnificent cover!

They can be reached at: http://theempowermentduo.com

www.ingramcontent.com/pod-product-compliance
Lightning Source LLC
Chambersburg PA
CBHW070309230526
45470CB00002B/792